DOGS SET VIII

WEIMARANERS

Jill C. Wheeler

ABDO Publishing Company

visit us at
www.abdopublishing.com

Published by ABDO Publishing Company, 8000 West 78th Street, Edina, Minnesota 55439.
Copyright © 2010 by Abdo Consulting Group, Inc. International copyrights reserved in
all countries. No part of this book may be reproduced in any form without written
permission from the publisher. The Checkerboard Library™ is a trademark and logo of
ABDO Publishing Company.

Printed in the United States of America, North Mankato, Minnesota.
092009
012010

Cover Photo: Alamy
Interior Photos: Alamy pp. 5, 7, 10, 11, 21; AP Images pp. 9, 13; Corbis p. 19;
iStockphoto pp. 14–15; Peter Arnold p. 17

Series Coordinator: Tamara L. Britton
Editors: Tamara L. Britton, Heidi M.D. Elston
Art Direction: Neil Klinepier

Library of Congress Cataloging-in-Publication Data

Wheeler, Jill C., 1964-
Weimaraners / Jill C. Wheeler.
    p. cm. -- (Dogs)
Includes index.
ISBN 978-1-60453-785-7
1. Weimaraner (Dog breed)--Juvenile literature. I. Title.
SF429.W33W53 2010
636.752--dc22

CONTENTS

THE DOG FAMILY

In the wild or in the house, all dogs belong to the **Canidae** family. This name comes from the Latin word *canis*, which means "dog." Members of the Canidae family include foxes, coyotes, and wolves.

The **domestic** dog's closest relative is the gray wolf. In fact, all dogs are descendants of wolves. The first dogs were wolves that began living with humans to help them hunt.

Eventually, people began to **breed** dogs for the features they found most appealing. The Weimaraner was developed in Germany. This sporting dog was bred to assist hunters in the field.

Weimaraners

WEIMARANERS

The Weimaraner is a relatively young **breed**. It dates back to the early 1800s. The dogs were first known as Weimar pointers. They were named after Weimar, an area in what is now Germany.

Weimaraners were bred for bravery, **endurance**, speed, and **tracking**. Early Weimaraners hunted wolves, deer, and bears. Over time, there were fewer large game animals in Germany. The Weimaraner adapted to hunt birds and smaller game animals instead.

Weimar nobles had sponsored the Weimaraner's breeding program. They wanted to protect the Weimaraner's bloodlines. So, they formed the German Weimaraner Club. Only club members could own Weimaraners.

6

Weimaraners are excellent hunting dogs. They have natural pointing and retrieving abilities.

Then in 1928, an American named Howard Knight became a member of the club. Ten years later, Knight began a Weimaraner breeding program in the United States. The **American Kennel Club (AKC)** recognized the breed in 1943.

7

WHAT THEY'RE LIKE

Weimaraners are fearless, friendly, obedient, and alert. The dogs are so friendly that some have become service dogs. They assist people with disabilities. Others have served as rescue dogs.

Properly trained Weimaraners make excellent members of the family pack. They are loyal and devoted family members. These fun-loving dogs enjoy playing with both children and adults.

Weimaraners are full of energy and eager to learn. They can be trained to participate in dog sports. These include **agility** competitions and **tracking**. Such activities provide good exercise for these active dogs.

The first dog agility course was created for the 1978 Crufts Dog Show in England.

COAT AND COLOR

Weimaraners are sometimes called Grey Ghosts. This is because of their short, smooth, sleek, gray coat. The shades of gray can range from blue gray to silver gray. Often, the coat is a lighter gray on the head and the ears. Weimaraners sometimes have a splash of white on their chests.

Some Weimaraners have long hair. Fans of this coat type tried to get the **AKC** to recognize long-haired Weimaraners.

A long-haired Weimaraner

That effort failed. Still, long- and short-haired Weimaraner puppies can be born in the same **litter**. And, kennel clubs in other countries do recognize the long coat.

Long or short, Weimaraner coats shed. However, they do not shed any more than the average dog. The short coat is low maintenance. It should be brushed with a firm-bristle brush once or twice a week.

A short-haired Weimaraner

11

SIZE

Weimaraners are medium-sized dogs. Males stand between 25 and 27 inches (63 and 69 cm) tall. Females are slightly smaller. They stand 23 to 25 inches (58 to 63 cm) tall. Adult dogs weigh between 70 and 85 pounds (32 and 39 kg).

Weimaraners are graceful, balanced dogs. They have a long head and long, hanging ears. Their backs are long and straight, as are their legs. The dogs have well-developed muscles. The **docked** tail is about six inches (15 cm) long.

Weimaraners were **bred** to spend lots of time outdoors. However, they do not like to live outside. This makes them a fairly large indoor dog breed.

Award-winning artist William Wegman with his Weimaraners Batty (left) and Chip. Wegman's art often features his dogs and has made the breed more popular.

CARE

Weimaraners are energetic sporting dogs. They need more exercise than many other **breeds**. A full day of activity is no problem for them. They were bred to hunt all day!

If your Weimaraner is a hunting dog, check its coat for ticks after outings. It is also a good idea to regularly clean the dog's feet. Weimaraners have webbed feet. This helps them to be better swimmers. However, the space between their toes can harbor harmful debris.

It is important to check your dog's eyes, nose, mouth, and skin often. A good time to do this is when grooming the coat. A dog's teeth should be brushed daily. Its nails should be trimmed regularly, too.

14

Weimaraners can develop health concerns, such as hip problems. A veterinarian can help keep your Weimaraner healthy. He or she can **spay** or **neuter** your dog. The veterinarian can also provide regular exams and **vaccines**.

Regular checkups will protect against illness.

FEEDING

There are several types of dog foods available. The most popular are dry, moist, and semimoist. The veterinarian can recommend the right diet for your Weimaraner.

The amount of food a dog needs will depend on activity level and age. New puppies should eat two to three times a day. Owners should feed older puppies and adult dogs twice a day.

Pay attention to your dog after it has eaten. Weimaraners can have problems with **bloat**. This condition can be fatal if not treated quickly.

Owners can help their dogs avoid bloat. One way is to feed them several small meals instead of one large meal. This way, the dog will not become very hungry and gulp its food. And don't forget, all dogs need lots of fresh water available at all times.

A high-quality food will provide the most nutrition for the money.

THINGS THEY NEED

Weimaraners like to exercise outdoors with their families. Hiking, playing ball, and walking through fields are favorite activities.

At home, a large, fenced-in backyard provides a safe place to exercise. If not fenced in, the Weimaraner may wander off looking for something to hunt. If Weimaraners do not get enough exercise outside, they will try to get it inside!

Weimaraners need strong leadership. They should have clear limits on what they are allowed to do. Owners must be prepared to spend a lot of time with their Weimaraner. If left alone for long periods, these dogs can become restless and destructive.

All Weimaraners should have a collar, a license, and identification tags. Toys can help keep these active dogs busy. A bed provides a soft, warm place to rest. This loyal **breed** also needs a loving family, **socialization**, and training. Meeting these needs will result in a happy, well-behaved pet.

Weimaraners are loyal and devoted to the people they love.

PUPPIES

Weimaraners are **pregnant** for about 63 days. Then, they give birth to about six puppies. The puppies need to stay with their mother for eight to twelve weeks. Then, a loving family can adopt them.

If a Weimaraner is right for your family, look for a reputable **breeder**. When choosing your pet, look for playful and curious puppies. They should be willing to approach people and be held.

A Weimaraner puppy needs to begin training as soon as it joins the household. Owners should use a crate for the puppy to help with house-training. This also protects furniture and belongings from the puppy's teeth!

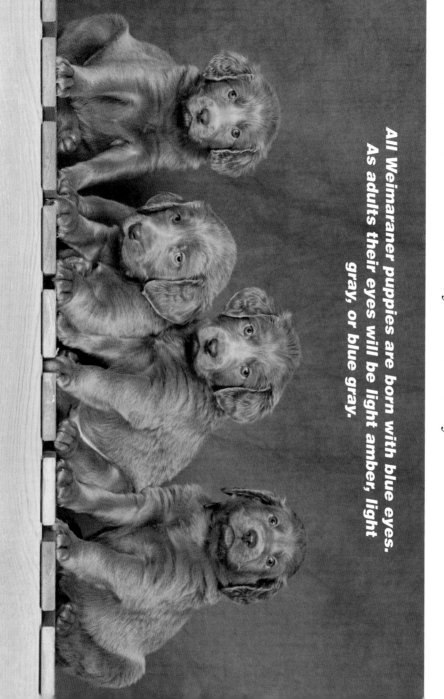

All Weimaraner puppies are born with blue eyes. As adults their eyes will be light amber, light gray, or blue gray.

Introduce your new puppy to different experiences, animals, and people right away. This will help it grow into a well-adjusted dog. Properly trained and cared for Weimaraners can be happy members of the family for 10 to 12 years.

GLOSSARY

agility - a sport in which a handler leads a dog through an obstacle course during a timed race.

American Kennel Club (AKC) - an organization that studies and promotes interest in purebred dogs.

bloat - a condition in which food and gas trapped in a dog's stomach cause pain, shock, and even death.

breed - a group of animals sharing the same ancestors and appearance. A breeder is a person who raises animals. Raising animals is often called breeding them.

Canidae (KAN-uh-dee) - the scientific Latin name for the dog family. Members of this family are called canids. They include domestic dogs, wolves, jackals, foxes, and coyotes.

docked - cut short.

domestic - tame, especially relating to animals.

endurance - the ability to sustain a long, stressful effort or activity.

22

litter - all of the puppies born at one time to a mother dog.

neuter (NOO-tuhr) - to remove a male animal's reproductive organs.

pregnant - having one or more babies growing within the body.

socialize - to accustom an animal or a person to spending time with others.

spay - to remove a female animal's reproductive organs.

tracking - a sport in which a dog follows a scent trail to locate a person or an object.

vaccine (vak-SEEN) - a shot given to animals or humans to prevent them from getting an illness or a disease.

WEB SITES

To learn more about Weimaraners, visit ABDO Publishing Company on the World Wide Web **www.abdopublishing.com.** Web sites about Weimaraners are featured on our Book Links page. These links are routinely monitored and updated to provide the most current information available.

INDEX